DIRT RICH

Graeme Richardson grew up in Nottinghamshire, and now lives and works in Germany. A former Chaplain and Fellow of Brasenose College, Oxford, he has also served as a Parish Priest in Hertfordshire and Birmingham. Over the last twenty years, his writing has featured in various publications including the *Guardian* and the *Times*, and he has been a regular contributor to the *Times Literary Supplement* since 2010. A first pamphlet, *Hang Time*, was published in 2006 from Landfill Press; his second pamphlet, *Last of the Coalmine Choirboys* came out in 2024 from New Walk Editions. Since 2022 he has been Poetry Critic for the *Sunday Times*.

CARCANET POETRY

DIRT RICH

GRAEME RICHARDSON

First published in Great Britain in 2026 by
Carcanet
Main Library, The University of Manchester
Oxford Road, Manchester, M13 9PP
www.carcanet.co.uk

A CIP catalogue record for this book is
available from the British Library.

ISBN 978 1 80017 534 1

Book design by Andrew Latimer, Carcanet
Typesetting by LiteBook Prepress Services
Printed in Great Britain by SRP Ltd, Exeter, Devon

MIX
Paper | Supporting
responsible forestry
FSC   FSC® C014540
www.fsc.org

The publisher acknowledges financial
assistance from Arts Council England.

Supported using public funding by
ARTS COUNCIL
ENGLAND

CONTENTS

I

II

III

IV

for Jeremy Noel-Tod

Out of the glacial night,
Out of the long cave quiet,
First you see only light;
Following, you see by it.

I

Nothing so complete as missing a train.
No half measures. It's over, it happened.
Cut. The deserted half-dry platform, and,
over its roof, the day-intincted moon.
Turn to the calming gallery of smiles.
More pictures of one girl aged six than of
my father over his eighty-three years.
His parents believed in heaven, being
themselves for ever. Their parents, in turn,
believed in hell and eternal torment,
the self repeatedly degraded but
never allowed to rest. I dared to look
through spittle-fleck this morning, as I shaved.
Redoubts, cavities, stubble, and shadows
under the skin, an inward bellying
of smoke, grey as a wasp's nest. It happened.
Lazarus, patron saint of latecomers,
pray for me, you who were condemned to live
knowing what we go through to die, knowing
what it takes, nevertheless, to get up
every clawed-down morning and start again,
step back from the empty freight-train stampede
in time for the cloud of powdery snow
that whirls and reels and marvels in its wake,
commuting the grave-clothes into thin air.

ROLEX OYSTER PERPETUAL BOMBE

Posh end of the next parish
(hadn't the heart to say no);
mock-tudor, privet;
Porsches, porches.
Rain not discouraging
tasteful blackbirds
in pollarded trees.
Loose-leaf tea
in fine bone-china, tray
perched on a fringed pouffe.
Rattling around a six-
bedroom detached,
the widow insisted
I bury with his ashes
his most precious worldly good.
Bought '63. Never worn.
Who else would want it?
Couldn't you sell it? Oh
I don't need the money. See?
He'd coo over that in its box.

Mixed with the gravelly
hilltop earth, and coarse-milled
previous owner, it hunkers,
sparkling condition
dimming with each second
of worm-delighting downpour.
Google it: eighteen-carat
yellow gold case, case-back;
original fluted bezel
and lugs; high quality

brown Morellato leather strap
with gold-plated buckle.
In the Vicarage, I seethe.
The baby cries every hour
on the dot. The graveyard owl
sarcastically responds.
The answer to all
our problems
still going but stuck.
I swear I can hear it tick.

BEARINGS

One poor dear – 84, in the hospice,
just a few picked chicken-bones
under the sheets, fists
bulbs of dried garlic,
and a head of dandelion fluff
almost blown –
before she finally gave up
cried out all night for her Mum.

Sometimes my kids cry out for me.
Easier to get out of bed, though,
than to get out of sleep.
I can't get my bearings.
Where can they be?
Where has the door gone?

IN HOLYWELL CEMETERY

Swirling iron, craquelure and rust,
shuddering with slowly crawling cars.
Earth absorbs the poison with the dust;
graves await an amaranthine grass.

Tourists come to look for Kenneth Grahame's,
noting that it first contained his son.
Elder covers up the single names,
Heberden and Pater overrun.

Study a disaster, love a grief.
Trying to make it better makes it worse.
Restoration left to a naïf
brandishing the bluntest secateurs.

Loving without knowing isn't love.
Knowing without loving is half-known.
Lovers know they never know enough.
Scholars know they end up here alone.

So, through love or wisdom, we perform
homage to what's dead as though we must.
Sunset glows against the coming storm:
swirling iron, craquelure and rust.

DEATH OF AN ARISTOTELIAN

The brain was drained of oxygen.
The parsing jaw grew weak.
No spectacles or dentures.
The nose became a beak.

The book-lined room was gloomy,
The conifers leaned in,
neglected thickets needing
their own dose of Warfarin.

Returning from the hospital,
they made his bed downstairs.
And there he lay, surrounded
by his ancestors and heirs.

The house now worth a million,
his children gathered round.
But was he gone? They stroked his hand.
They spoke. He made no sound.

Our foremost commentator
on the Nicomachean Ethics,
he had no time for bloviating
muddle (the Poetics)

and metaphysics bored him.
He always used to say
the only prayer worth knowing
was the prayer said at A.A.

But even for philosophers
a time of no control
is coming, when we're haunted
by the spectre of the soul.

The chaplain on a rusty bike
came panting up the drive.
The expert in the College
on who was still alive.

But dark was the barometer,
and dark the parquet floor,
and dark the narrow serving-hatch,
and dark the fanlight door.

And just as he opined and dined
through countless Oxford terms,
the Master tipped his head back,
as one that begs for worms.

FOLLY ISLAND SONG
(for Harry Judge)

Hellebores and Cyclamen,
bed-bound, droop and shiver.
Herons wait like highwaymen
for the Thames to stand and deliver.
The bank's policed by gulls and geese,
but light plays free on the river.

Coaches deride an eight's technique,
lecturers sit and mark,
bike-brakes on the towpath shriek,
dogs and their drunkards bark.
The tourists must return to their bus
but the river will dance till dark.

Round the city, traffic clogs
ring-road and motorway;
idiot drive-time monologues
tell of the same delay;
But the geese that fly through a darkening sky
know the river was free all day.

The river was free all day.

SUFFOLK BOY

(i.m. Chris Richardson)

Your stony grey beach is bleak and dull
as colliery slag-heaps or High Peak scree.
But the more you look the more you see
individuals, various, colourful.

Out of the rubble, a slow flowering
of lavender- lilac- heather-greys.
Jumble rewards the undaunted gaze,
attention being a sort of Spring,

another reminder that wonder works.
Just so, by watching, you learnt to swim,
and found the best kind of pebble to skim,
Coralline Crag and quartzite pucks,

so making a line through crests and plumes,
that even when sinking seemed the end,
the sea could reverse the verdict of land:
a stone that rises, a burden that blooms.

ONE MORE LAST WORD FROM THE CROSS
(i.m. Matt Carver)

Cream in the coffee tumbles and writhes;
exhaust-pipes in the road-side's
blackened gravel twist and turn;
the river's gut-feelings of fear and revulsion
send it running from the town
as I run from you.

Smokers in drizzle dip a toe in the water;
with cortisone injections, England's
hope of glory, out in the middle,
battles on; westward bound,
roads and their roadkill lie open:
I open to you.

Dead-weight tonnage, the church towers
over the town, a great cloud.
I park under chestnut trees.
His family at the lych-gate
standing, they couldn't say how.
And I stand for you.

Keening, those chestnuts lurch and sway;
bowling through the pain
the river guides him home;
we enter the cloud and stand in its smoke
as it tumbles and writhes.
You say:

I am the Resurrection and the Life.

ROBINIA PSEUDOACACIA

As one who falls every day
through trapdoors yet never feels
the rope stand tight I salute
these leaves that drop so lightly
they flip-flop on helices
invisible and gentle,
land calmly, curl up, succumb.

This is stock of that same world
of fever, bull-market fear;
figment currencies teem and
dissolve; but this lovely shade
no-one can hold dies in hope:
in gold so fresh it looks green
and green so rich it looks gold.

WOODSMOKE

I shall be walking past stark city gardens of October,
or, on a stringent winter's night, a hub of cottages, air
ice-burning the throat – and in seeps woodsmoke;

winding me up in its tar-sharpness, leading me
back to that farm-house, hired for its peace,
its log-fire that hissed, sighed, settled, glowing sleep,

whose smoke spooled out in the black, smoke
followed me out to the grass-crested lane, the track
going no place I drifted, full of a secret to savour –

you: that mouth with the moon open ready,
and heart with the plot open ready, and eyes wide,
lifted with poplars in moonlight, ready and open.

Maybe I'll see you, twenty years later, in London –
still lit, still lighting, that lodestar spark –
but the labyrinth-thread in my fingers just smoke.

LEMON PIP

Nestled in acid,
in fine sprays of bitterness,
in a wincing air-kiss
you are spat out,
or spurt from plucking,
niggle at hangnails,
hamper and devil
cocktails and cakes.
Sharp as a fish-bone,
broad-bean-waxy,
elusive as a name
or the earliest dream,
you doss around
the squeezer's dome,
grey-green, wizened;
as if you once lived,
pink and hearty
and cradled:
a zestling.

II

MANSFIELD NOTTS

Stand outside the old sandstone school – St. John's. Look around
at the battling terraced houses: square, solid, squat.
The road that snarls to the doorsteps, and the windows boarded-up,
and the furious scribble of briar, crossing-out a derelict lot.

When I was there, the mines made a brave attempt at colour and pride:
galas, banners, marching bands – even a majorette.
All talk was Thatcher and Scargill, but the Dukeries wouldn't strike
for a future they didn't believe in, and a past they'd best forget.

The earth being almost exhausted, they built in another direction:
pallets, skips, and scrap-yards; superstores, car-parks, flats;
the library with its lift, and its café on the top-floor,
and the blackberry bushes stretching up on the spoil-tip ziggurats.

Children stayed at the surface –– and these were their surfaces:
lacquered plywood, linoleum; the varnish of wheel-back chairs,
fake-oak kitchens, butterscotch tiles embossed with sheaves of wheat;
tortoise-shell scabs on jam-tart wounds from the burn of carpeted stairs.

I learnt about success. Success was surviving pain:
stabbing between our fingers with a compass-spike in maths.
Tears were always denied, the earliest self-betrayal,
blamed on cigarettes, or the chlorine of the public baths.

Pain stood firm in Leeming Street, and on the Bull Farm estate,
and by the Metal Box factory, and the gates of Thompson's grave;
in the bus-station's grimy concrete, or the subway's percussive tunnel;
out to King's Mill Hospital, and back to the Rock Hill caves.

The church was wholly different – the lychgate stopping cars,
and no commercial point to the narrow, impossible steeple,
or the carvings no-one could see, high in the walls and the roof,
and the green where no-one played, with its hillocks of sleeping people.

It was a mine of pain, in its sorrowing, sighing words,
painful for martyrs to understand and empires to misconstrue;
and its hero, the bloodied man descended into hell
who came up again good as new.

FOSSIL FUEL

In print on the lounge floor skin
seersucker from carpet pile,
folded limbs pressed into sleep.
Prehistory: the snuff movie.
Self-captive somehow, self-scared,
I knew I had to see more.

I'd settle on that one page:
asphalt pooled from gilsonite,
the tar pits of La Brea.
Tricked in, a giant sloth wails
as *smilodon fatalis*
chows down on its own last meal.

You died of wanting to live.
Even the far-sighted hawks
were doomed to struggle and snap,
and bow their head to the hood,
the tar their master – like time,
one vast muscle and gullet.

Wells of Artex gurgled.
Walls with subsidence cracked.
I scrabbled to turn the page,
a sabre-tooth on my back,
as ceiling-shadow raptors
swept over the mire, the trap.

The reconstruction looks tired:
Primitive Boy With His Books.
Yet to be smiled on by fate;
not yet woeful carrion.
I pause, in the museum.
I try to imagine him.

HISTORY TEACHING
(for my mother)

Fly in resin can't get free
saved by the blood of the redwood tree.

If I forget you, don't you forget me.

Ageing but not moving we
are locked in lonely infancy.

If I forget you, don't you forget me.

One says it last. Who will it be?
Amber waits in a glittering sea.

If I forget you, don't you forget me.

THE CEMENT FACTORY

An aqualung in concrete and brick
abandoned by the bypass
on a seabed of littered fields.
Hedges catch as kelp catches;
in them, scraps of jellyfish plastic
flutter and moan, and stay years.

Before, when it was used,
it still looked wrecked and derelict.
Vans and battered pick-ups
bounded the pot-holes out of it,
invisible men at the wheel,
floating tattoos and singlets.

The size was always a decoy –
inside there's nothing to it,
a pigeon-coop, a magic lantern
of wings, blistered, stucco
of damp and crap, the streaky
walls a melted barcode.

Why would you loiter here?
Labour is done and gone.
Why would you stoop, and step
over the twisted rods?
A house for the broken in ruins;
for binding and filling, empty.

But back with the slingshot pulleys
and cogs, those fossil crowns,
where flailing circles end –
there, the spilled-out memory lies,
for any trespasser to find,
of what held everything fast.

UNLATCHED AND LIT

*(for the Choirs of St Peter and St Paul,
Mansfield and St Peter's, Harborne)*

This sanctuary of my soul
at midnight is a seam of coal,
packed with power but hard to break.
I mine it as I lie awake.

Pixellated, hassock-wool
Angel, Lion, Eagle, Bull;
cobweb-fur in every lock,
stained-glass windows' dull mock-croc;

crossed keys, swords, reclining stags,
on the rafters' tattered flags
gossamer as candle-smoke
rising under Sherwood oak;

on deep sills, in each chipped vase,
Oasis stinks beneath the flowers;
countered by the vestry's whiff
of Brasso, beeswax, Vim and Jif.

All those stories – common, once,
lost sheep, lost coin, and then lost sons –
whisper to a heavenly host
of woodworm, rats, and plaintive ghosts.

Here, before these well-worn pews,
children walked in polished shoes
unsteadily processing in
and never coming out again.

THOSE AMIABLE DWELLINGS

Not for the last time, I needed my sight corrected.
Dettol-sting tears in cushioned corridors.
Humbled by the hospital's backless patterned gown.
Doctors on their rounds gave nurses instructions:
touch and go – touch and go.

First time on my own. I took flight to my dug-outs and bunkers:
Harlow Wood dell of yellow-flowered gorse, or
those snug enclosed hollows, the den
in the hillside's rogue rhododendron, escaped
from a local stately home.

That landscape, butchered and gouged by industry –
Ratcher Hill Quarry, Ling Forest, Thieves Wood –
was a glittering reservoir, for those who know the trick,
who going through the vale of misery use it for a well
and the pools are full of water.

I tried to recall whole psalms and descants.
The weekend way to Strawberry Knob.
Hawthorn and heather. Ash-grey soil.
The golden oak-leaves got the light, and the darkness
comprehended it not.

Coke-furnace sunset in Clipstone Forest.
The headstocks grazing peacefully in the distance.
Before the sponsored walk, Dad would drive us round,
marking out the route with sawdust arrows,
Sports Report on the radio.

I cried for my mum, but was told that wouldn't do.
I tried a low whistle of 'Brother James's Air'.
I thought of our arrows marking the track,
starting off clumsy, peaking in the middle, then
tailing off, becoming slapdash.

I woke, and wore an eye-patch for a week.
Flesh-coloured, soft, though. Hardly piratical.
I remembered acutely the torments of the ward,
and knew it was one of those things you never
speak of but store securely away.

When I stand on the edge of another black pit,
I make the same journey, give the same recital.
The choir's no more. The hospital bulldozed.
The dell replaced by 'quality housing'. Gorse and heather
pulled up with the roots.

But the dove came back at least once to the ark
with nothing, before that triumphant olive-leaf.
In the dwindling forest, I sift out sawdust from my fist:
grain that unless it falls to the ground and dies
remains alone.

EARTHBOUND AND DOWN

The Challenger Disaster hit our playground
in a shower of reprehensible jokes:
NASA stands for 'Need Another Seven Astronauts'.
What's a spaceman's favourite drink? Seven Up.
Same as Snow White, said Danny Speed.
He and his older brother Craig were genius
engineers of the winter ice-slide, buffing
and polishing from just after dawn, a smear
of Vicks Vaporub over the frosty schoolyard.
No shoes with a grip or ridged sole allowed.
You scrambled hard then froze with the ice,
stillness carrying you further and faster
than movement ever could. Grounded flight.
Adults wanted unearthly beauty but to me
it was humdrum: Mozart's 'Ave Verum'
was something I'd rehearse as I plunged
on my Raleigh Milk Race down Berry Hill Road.
I wanted the opposite: I was asking the earth.
Eating a girl out, Craig once said, was to slip
into warmed-up Angel Delight, almost
unbelievably frictionless, the perfect slide.
My lunchbox full of tongue-sandwiches,
I hid them in gorse and watched them rot,
the same bush that yielded *Readers' Wives*,
find of the century, pages stuck together.
Grey fur grew on the lolling, folded meat.
Much later, Danny went down for dealing:
whizz, mostly – amphetamines – his surname
meaning he made it to the national news.
I saw it. He got years. We all got years.

God, the perils of the flesh were tiring. At the peak of my mania I found it therapeutic to hoover the cathedral (not a euphemism). It had to be done in the morning, before the arrival of gockles and gawpers. Already it was hot but that building was a cavernous fridge. The machine I dragged along was the last of its kind, a clanking metal pachyderm on wheels. As it trundled, roaring, over the Norman slabs, I struggled to control the enormous throbbing nozzle. Put your back into it, the Verger would chuckle, you're doing God's work.

Hark how the heavenly anthem drowns all music but its own. Dust and loose threads mustered in corners, cute furry creatures I half-expected to scurry away before my probing. I sucked them up with glee. Spiders in their rigging fought back in the hurricane, but they too eventually succumbed. Shed skin and Sunday-best lint formed little drifts on the chancel steps. There must be enough DNA here, I thought, to conjure up Frankenstein's Congregant and lead him to the font. One day he could take over the hoovering.

Tick tock in heels, a lady came to say an encouraging word. I saw the small damp hairs at her neck. 'I should be out in the garden in my bikini,' she said. Oh Christ. Just then, a buzz, a flapping sound. A coin? A scattered pearl? Or just a bearded jelly-baby? Quickly I slapped that red button, the size of a macaroon. But with the vacuum cleaner off, the sound continued. I stepped back. Everyone peered at the heavens.

Up by a clerestory window, a trapped blackbird hovered. An expert in praise, for whom every black hole can become a singing wine-glass, in sunlight ascending and descending, beyond all reason. Born for this, from the breakthrough of hatching, fluttering at that glory, a frenzied tongue.

Nothing doing, I turned the machine back on. Show them what you're made of, son.

PITHEAD

Lady – bear with me now –
here's an old miner's tale of woe
that somehow, through the years
of continual warring grimness,
my absent-minded lies
and empty-headed idiocies,
I've not forgotten.
Those stories had the same aim.
Practical jokes, horseplay in the shower –
the most important part of all that gear
was the coping mechanism.
That, and the snap-tin.
Snap left out, you're asking for it,
pit-ponies would snaffle it,
fond of a jam sandwich, snatch it
even from the pocket of your jacket.
And this, I used to love hearing:
a tired and barkled collier returned
to his coat once and found
a pony had had his bloody orange.
You'd think it was safe in your duds.
But the bugger snuck his muzzle in,
such tender cunning, nuzzling
flesh and juice through the threads.
Buried life. Plodding the tunnels,
pulling tubs in skull-cap and bridle.
Who would deny him that sunburst dazzle –
all sweetness, and breezy fields?

LAST OF THE COALMINE CHOIRBOYS

With Evensong we buried him,
  The quick who loved the dead;
With ruff starched tight, and surplice white,
  And cassock royal red.

Responses were by Gibbons.
  The psalm-chant was by Smart.
Tchaikovsky's 'Hymn of the Cherubim'
  Followed 'As Pants The Hart'.

The echoes prized each beautifully
  Articulated word;
The diction crisp, no slur or lisp,
  Through canticles by Byrd.

But turn to the heavy Bible,
  Caress the ribbon down;
Though edged with gold, it's coarse and old,
  The corners torn and brown.

'Remember your creator
  While music's daughters strut
With golden bowl and pitcher whole
  And silver cords uncut.'

Turn to the New Testament,
  Turn over with a thud,
'The sun will wear sackcloth of hair,
  The moon will turn to blood'.

The coal was six feet thick there,
  The roof a foot of Coombe,
With air ablaze, the ripping face
  Became a rock-scaled tomb.

Why won't it come to the surface?
  The winding engines stall.
After an age, they send the cage
  Back down to clear the fall.

The photographs in the vestry
  Start off in sepia;
Then every shade begins to fade
  And ends an empty square.

Each blackened name on a gravestone,
  Each cross inscribed 'I AM',
Breaks from its base, falls on its face,
  And worships the White Lamb.

For faces they will fail me,
  And names I will forget,
But music sung when I was young
  Is sound within me yet.

Time is an ever-rolling stream
  But shallow, streaked with weeds.
In spate or drought, this rock stands out,
  And, cleft for me, it bleeds.

BRAMLEY SEEDLING

Stored winters apples'
breath on my face:
warmth in the cold.
A river unravels
to that orchard place
in the coalfield's fold,
to that brick box built
where the uprooted railway's
now a cinder track.
The years' black silt
was to bury me always
but I live. Take me back.

III

CHIAROSCURO

With acne by Seurat,
I was nonetheless outstandingly white,
quite the *Made im Speck*.
It was the look I was working on ('Keats,
Exiting the Funfair')
ghostly, elated, slightly sick.
When your family took me to the beach
they were stunned.

Of course you were syrup-brown.
Danish summers, sleeping-in till noon,
then strolling almost naked to the sea,
through almost naked sunlight in the wood.
In England the colours
all fading you must long to be free.
Not just the clothes hang
heavy on your shoulders;

we sleep through summer like stone.
But when, the other night,
you called me over,
and my fingers, my mouth,
remembered what they had by heart,
our two skins indistinct
in blackout hard-won –
I thought: let's die together.

FOR THE ALBUM

Our wedding-day, long tight in Kodak wallets,
sometimes splashes out all over again.

How I made my vows with unclean teeth;
how your hands were barren of flowers;
no-one had keys to anything.

All the while older women looked
for parallels, history, romance.

Your air-raid grip on my hand.

Standing and smiling, a small-town alderman,
I have my own undeveloped snaps:

that building-site outside our flat
(we waited for a taxi to our own reception);

the heavens, your dress, in the same blue puddle;
bricks stacked smart, and the mud in plaits.

AFTER THE DEATH OF A CHILD

I — A PASTORAL HECKLE

The dead live on in memory? Not true.
They lodge there dead, and yours not theirs the hell.
The world without them waits, besieging you;
Their corpse within you, poisoning the well.
That body was, by all your senses, known,
with knowledge more acute now 'it' is ash.
The rescuer, sent out, returns alone,
and relic-hunters come to you with trash,
and every consolation seems a lie:
no letting be, no love in letting go,
no harvest in a void; the sun has gone
to pieces in the song-forsaken sky,
and night withdraws the way; and you don't know
how – *thank you, yes, it's ten years* – you live on.

II — A VISITATION

Standing at my bedside, as your ghost,
you wake me; ask; and in you get,
body slammed on the sheet, hair moist
at the temples; nose, ears, wet;
born into my deep night's warmth,
a foal in amniotic mess,
I lick you clean. I nurse.
It will not sweep you off, this storm.

Frailty of all we have – cracked house,
and creaking bed;
darkness makes it obvious,
and you cry for the lonely dead
who lie like you, pressed:
by weight of vacant air, or depth of dirt;
like you beyond all comfort;
but they rest.

III — SOUND THE RETREAT

I find her dying; with panicked breath,
she recognizes and lets in death.

The fence she died on still shook.
Slowly I walk each week to look.

First the eye is still black and bright:
a windscreen under a street-light.

Then the flesh of the head and neck's
stripped: sheath from flex.

Then the mound of the body collapses:
the lancing of an abscess.

Finally all that's left is a hoof,
compact, sturdy, weather-proof,

still caught in the fence-wire's mesh,
the black pad springy and fresh.

And you, who found and startled her,
with lifted and electric fur,

the one so quiet behind the door
hunts you too – you know what for.

Amend the liturgies. Footnote the books.
The hart never reaches the water-brooks.

c90s

Slyly, idly, I look for her online;
sleepless, tossed from my own bed by a scream.
But she eludes enlargements of the screen
(could that be her? Fatter now, saturnine,
grimacing under a strange married name?)
and shame needs no updates. Picture the scene:

every cloud had flowered into cornflower blue
over the meadow's old lace, late snow.
Water ran off clear. April would be warm.
I got this from a book, but was it true?
(Except by saying it, how could I know?)
I am at rest with you, I have come home.

What was she like then? Never alone.
Her youngish mother gave her older tastes
in clothes, music, men... And gave her mix-tapes,
marked in fading biro, off-white as bone –
they soothed her, a baby, full-lipped, round-faced,
surprised by her own mess, her own mistakes.

I threw them out, those reliquary songs:
cassettes of white-appropriated blues
whose bobbins, turning, turned each other on
until one stalled, and, so far strung along,
the other sent disconsolate lassoes
that crumpled up, all magnetism down,

no rest, nor home, not now. At 4am –
pop-ups of sites too toxic to visit,
the browser's freeze a feature not a glitch,
memory full – there it is, here I am.
One beggar's moment out of the blizzard.
That wide blue sky. Those paths. That crystal ditch.

TO THE QUICK

Drank a quart of whisky neat.
Hoped to drop. Stayed on my feet.

Used the mirror by my bed
every morning: still not dead.

Talked at friends, hour after hour,
calmly logical, if sour.

Felt no damage, felt no pain,
however loudly I'd complain.

But time is sharp: only that
cut from the heart its veil of fat.

ALBERT BRIDGE

After the December rush-hour
of mucous coughs and diesel-fumes,
two sparkling halves, one in the Thames,
one out, became a chandelier.

Like some Parisian brasserie,
shining in a cobbled back-street,
the cables, with their fairy-lights,
called out to every city stray.

Remember those winter Fridays?
The low-budget revels: to stroll
to the toll-booths that took no toll,
the languid obsidian waters.

So we walked through Chelsea, down Cheyne
Gardens, pretending to be rich,
to make out, on that blazing bridge,
all the paste baubles of London:

they saw you back home to my couch.
Now a shared photo on my phone
and, for a week, the bright vision
ripples again, just out of reach.

I know the end will be ruin,
that rivets scream and pillars drown.
Still – come for me, as you would then,
with nothing but your jewellery on.

ALL TOO MUCH AND NEVER ENOUGH

The grandfather had duelling-scars
on top of his bald head, he was so short.
The father was smuggled out of Karlsbad
in '45 in a rucksack.
His father once beat him with a cane
until he wet himself. Aged 14.
Both were, everyone agreed,
excellent doctors.

The house, a mod-con *Almhütte,*
with a view of the fairy-tale castle,
has many mansions. The flats
in Kiel and Aarhus; the Baltic yacht;
the island beach-house; and the farm
by the shallow, gloomy fjord,
where a solitary wind turbine
gestured helplessly to the bay:

the contents of all are here.
An excess of crockery; lamps;
champagne-flutes in five different shapes;
flabby piles of mismatched towels
and unworn waffle bathrobes.
Books on hunting and boats
get more out-of-tune each year
like the white beach-house piano.

In the many, many drawers,
repose the forgotten mothers.
The father's, buck-toothed in a *Strandkorb*,
who died when he was six;
her successor, monstrous in furs.
The step-mother takes pride of place;
pushing, towards the lens,
her infernally glowing pubic hair.

Of the outcast mother, nothing
but silhouettes of the heads
of her daughters, in a corner,
where old coats flop on the exercise-bike,
just to the left of the gun-safe,
sure at the heart of the house,
a priest-hole with its priest
all set for the Last Rites.

BUST

In Weimar, failed artists and lovers
ensconce themselves in cafés.

On Herderplatz, they plead:
a right spirit can be renewed.

In Park an der Ilm, the gardener
boards-up the statues for winter

against the bitter frost:
Sándor Petőfi, Shakespeare, Liszt

each in a fortified house.
In spring, when the gingko flowers,

he gingerly lays bare the stone.
What if it was broken all along?

GENESIS

A burp-caw, croak-bark chorale:
the palace lily-pond froths with life,
good head, brimming with spawn
and sticky weed. We brought
the kids here to listen but they talk
(someone has to) into the general din:
scores of lounging amphibian
love-pats, bubbling in the sun.

Once upon such an uproarious time
sides split and we were born,
one flesh in exaltation.
Hands off said all good sense
but we would not obey,
not in that humidity, in the cause
of greenness redeemed and all nature
coming into bud in those same hands.

Now, I carry the coats and wet-wipes,
and you attend to their targets,
and *ooh* and *aah* at fireworks
of japonica and laburnum.
You are mad now, frogs, but your song
beckons a flood of such grief
it will carry you away, even as you call
a far ark, a far ark.

ETERNITIES

'Not having you in my life is like going back
to time, after once living in eternity.'
– Stanley Spencer (in a letter to his wife)

Hours refusing to pass
tyrannize my days.
As a stray inside the pound
yowls to roam and range,
I mither at the glass,
cursing another phase
of watch-hands teasing round
or light feinting to change.

Then why isn't memory
a catalogue of the hours
when boredom became a call,
a song, an insistent rhyme?
Instead, and so vividly,
the time that was solely ours
is what remains, after all,
and never felt like time.

IV

SEVERNSIDE CHERRY

At the height of the heatwave,
when the car's steel gave lesions and grazes
at a standstill, we headed for the hills;
tense in traffic, a legion behind its shields,
then breaking out to the back-roads,
we crossed a river dragged away by its heels,
reaching, just as the satnav succumbed,
polytunnels, orchards –– a fruit farm.

Almost everything was gone;
rows the hopeful rambled down
bare shelves, bulbless lamps,
the duds pulped in dust.
They said the cherry fields were still alright
a mile or so up the lane – but it felt
three or four, heat
reopening the tarmac's scars.

On my chest a desert crocus I carried you;
and you slept hot, at work
in that crucible; I wielded your glow,
a comic-book heat-ray
melting the weary woman I asked
for directions, her children were bored now,
inferior, formed, eating more than they paid for.
I smooched your fresh damp drowsy head.

Finally the turn came round;
and most of the trees were scrunched-up
waste-paper holding nothing;
we went past crowds to a far foreign corner

and there, three trees in,
the one that got away, one that not only
survived but sang, a sparkling
blood aria, a saint on fire.

Rare in these days, but how ripe things
shrug themselves into your hands,
hug themselves in their punnets –
you never forget. Spring to my lips;
give me a double portion of your zest.
Let the sun's yield be respite from the heat.
Let no-one die of their bruises.
Baby let me sleep your summer-noon sleep.

STILL

About the soothing,
hugging, rocking; the
night-waking, teething,
the cluster-feeding:
truthfully, sometimes,
your demands, your needs,
seem unreasonable.
So too my response –
I clamp and stifle,
sing and talk-over,
swing, pat and shuffle
round the blacked-out room.

Should I sit you down
in a high-backed chair,
and prompt, head inclined,
calmly listening?
And, to your radish-
faced howls and shrieking,
tactfully gesture
at the tissue-box;
after a pause, ask
how that made you feel;
nod as you convulse,
huff-snuffle in grief?

No, I shush – rain
in a rainforest,
leaf-swish and branch-brush,
ape-balm, parrot-hush,
leopard-lullaby;

or push, through my teeth,
an ocean to shale
and pale midnight cliffs;
I put my old shell
to your shell-like, while
reason's not enough:
that rising tide's love.

SHORT DAY

Small footprints in snow –
so perfect – soon
will fade and go,
like the dawn winter moon.

Like the smudge moon at dawn
in low bleach sun:
only just born
but away you run.

You run far away
with the patter of thaw.
Your whole being play
and my heart sore.

BABY STEPS

You come forward, awed at finding your feet;
   queasily totter; then flail on one leg,
Chaplin cornering. The light breeze floors you,
   a horseshoe in its glove. You glare, get up,
go on, as easily led as water
   and, with limp tattered twigs and tiny rocks
in tight fistfuls, just as acquisitive.
   I watch. I almost blister as I wait.

You were the one we, spitting each midnight,
   moneyless, thought we would be forced to scotch.
You heard as whales hear a ship overturn,
   and persist in their deeps, and past them spears
and hooks dawdle, newly blind and inert.
   Now swallow the man of calamity
in that gummy all-wowing smile, drown his
   spine-song *(love and da-mage, love and da-mage)*.

I learnt about children from their mourners;
   in canteens where sugary tea congeals
while everyone tries to get their breath back
   and never will; or, in the viewing-room,
dim, net-curtained, peering over the edge
   of a small white box that's somehow also
a volcano unhinging its jaw; once
   blocking off the 'wrong' side, powdered black cracks

in the fixed young face; their faces crumple
   and fold like old pumpkins. Who willingly
would give their body to this quicklime hold?
   We could end up left behind. Your hand lifts
open, a crown splash of rain. I must pay.
   One strawberry-snail shell, and one acorn,
slit and sprouting in the fall: effigy
   and crude prototype. I fumble for change.

TOYS

Hunter of shipwrecks, I follow the debris trail;
kidnapper-quick, I chloroform the talking doll;
battlefield-ghoul, I tiptoe between the remains:
the Lego-shrapnel, the fallen Barbies and Kens.

Weariness, from the soles of the feet to the scalp.
Usual remedies, coffee or wine, don't help
with no problem being either woken or numb.
Just give me my orders in frantic, angry mime.

For fun, I imagine the scene when I'm knackered
for good: lying with gathered fragments by my bed,
at one with playthings long lost or loved to bits then.
Ah, the self-*fucking*-pity – my adrenalin!

Your 'borrowed' bouquets of roses billow like dust.
What if, Sweet Avalanche, this, in the end, sufficed?
Time's own rhythm of slip and grip, and in its sweep
all the charmed detritus it picks up. It picks up.

READY OR NOT

Progenitor and flunky,
  the maker made to wait,
I tut, and twirl the house-keys,
  reminding you you're late.

Late (you gurn in the mirror);
  late (you tell me a joke);
late (you mimic your sister);
  late (you love to provoke).

I kneel to do your boot-zip;
  you dance a one-legged jig
to your own babbling music.
  These boots were once too big –

and there: the familiar chill.
  Why do I wish away
time I want to stand still?
  Come on, stand still, I say.

AUBADE

Lost winning ticket found new every morning –
you say *don't squeeze too tight* but I gloat
over you – I exult, a dog beyond grabbing,
under a hedge, with the stolen Sunday roast;
I'm jubilant, that one desperate duck
who chainsaws through the crowd and swipes
the last piece of crust, and just as heedless
of the rest, the crestfallen, the starving standing by –
you are mine.

Too late I remember this is rush-hour –
where the pigeons start, and with them all
the piffling tasks of the week – a record-scratch take-off,
a falling-books flutter, a head-in-hands *Noooooo*
of spillage or breakage – every pause too short,
every ledge a rebuke of pins and goads…
Now, my pretty, we are at the school,
and this is by the crossing,
waiting for the light that says you can go.

A FAUNAL ASSEMBLAGE

The dawn flight was so cheap we could afford
to spend the night before at the airport,
in a hotel bed at nine pm all together:
baby, toddler, nursing mother, clueless father.

Lying on the sheets, sweaty and damp,
it felt like sinking in some prehistoric swamp,
the four of us, turning, interlocking limbs,
all of us breathing our different rhythms.

You could feel hard water flowing, cell by cell,
animal matter slowly becoming mineral,
the lack of oxygen meaning it was almost
forever before the bodies decomposed.

Historians will by guesswork recreate
exquisite things we hallow every day –
the baby's intricate alabaster nostrils,
the god-light captured in the toddler's curls –

and maybe not know specific insults and threats,
the tissue that degrades in scorn or stress,
that three were meant to take off on that flight
with one to watch them choked and petrified.

CHRISTMAS PRESENT

So I agreed to join in hide-and-seek,
despite being sleepy, awash with beer,
and at a disadvantage in physique,
but wanting to be present, to be *here*,
you know, to take away the mask, the screen,
and once again, at Christmas, be a kid.
The children counted backwards as I hid.
But then I saw, sat painfully between
two beds, their blankets balanced on my head,
that this – sit still, endure, don't speak a word –
is my adulthood: alien, exiled,
and worse, among pre-schoolers, well, pre-dead.
Then on that sad and lowly plain I heard
your laughter coming closer. Find me, child.

VIADUCT

Under the railway bridge, I think of jumping.
    Becoming,
        at that
          question-
        mark's
        low-
        point
        a

        dot.
Whip-zoom close-up head-shot of falling.
Result? Not exactly flattering.

Born in a mess, we die in a mess,
on a care-home's plastic cushions,
or a hospital's swiss-army bed,
peaks and troughs of our life a puddle –
why not flatten them here? Run over by
gravity, a truck full of grown-old grudges.

Someone has built a mini shrine.
Washed-out toys and pallid trinkets.
A line of plants. A little fence
that keeps no scavengers out.
Lugworm heaps of bird-shit.
A dagger-cross sunk deep.

You two wait, grinning on your bikes.
We look up to the vaulting bricks.
Hello, you shout – hell-low, hell-low.

Yours are the only answers.

REWILDING THE CHURCHYARD

Graves fall to the undergrowth
that broke the last good mower.
Cedars and self-seeders link
with the storm-forked sycamore.
Lime-leaves, sticky in the sun,
sprout from base and crown.

Sky jet-streaked, cloud-strewn.
On nettles, mellow with white bells,
open-book Cabbage Whites
marry their White Admirals.
Old Man's Beard and Queen Anne's Lace
in Catchweed, Bedstraw, Goosegrass.

This was our old haunt.
Without a better idea
of how to kill time, I used
to ramble with you here,
the grass so full and wild
over what time had killed.

The family names repeat, ever
more legibly in line.
You are the brightest, sharpest
engraving yet of mine,
illuminating each date,
an emissary of light.

Gloss of bottle-green beetle;
glaze of soil-ripple worms;
sheen of new Chinese marble
with familiar gold-leaf names
and plastic-wrapped bouquets
in the only tended place.

Now almost done with Poundland
magnifying-glass and jam-jar,
I'll lie under elder and ivy
where epitaphs disappear
and the holly grows shinier, higher,
through the hardstanding for the bier.

ACKNOWLEDGEMENTS

'Sound the Retreat', 'Woodsmoke', 'A Visitation', 'Severnside Cherry' and 'Ready or Not' first appeared in the *Times Literary Supplement:* thanks to Alan Jenkins and Camille Ralphs. 'Robinia Pseudoacacia' was published in the *Oxford Magazine:* thanks to Lucy Newlyn. 'Fossil Fuel' and 'Chiaroscuro' featured in *Areté:* thanks to Craig Raine. 'Still', 'Short Day', and 'Christmas Present' first appeared in *Bad Lilies:* thanks to Kathryn Gray and Andrew Neilson. 'For the Album' was in the pamphlet *Hang Time* from Landfill Press in 2006: thanks to Jeremy Noel-Tod. A selection of these poems was published in the 2024 *pamphlet Last of the Coalmine C\hoirboys* from New Walk Editions: thanks to Rory Waterman and Nick Everett.

Thanks to Michael Schmidt and John McAuliffe, and all those who read some of these poems in manuscript – especially Julia Copus, Matthew Francis, Kathryn Gray, Luke Kennard, Kay McCallum, Andrew Neilson, Jeremy Noel-Tod, Julius Purcell, Craig Raine, and Rory Waterman.